LEDGER

Jane Hirshfield was born in 1953 in New York City and received her A.B. from Princeton University in 1973. She has lived in northern California since 1974. In 2005 Bloodaxe Books published *Each Happiness Ringed by Lions: Selected Poems*, her first British publication, drawing on five award-winning American collections: *Alaya* (1982), *Of Gravity & Angels* (1988), *The October Palace* (1994), *The Lives of the Heart* (1997) and *Given Sugar, Given Salt* (2001). This was followed by four later collections from Bloodaxe in the UK: *After* (2006), a Poetry Book Society Choice shortlisted for the T.S. Eliot Prize; *Come, Thief* (2012); *The Beauty* (2015); and *Ledger* (2020). In 2008 Bloodaxe and Newcastle University published Jane Hirshfield's Newcastle/Bloodaxe Poetry Lectures, *Hiddenness, Surprise, Uncertainty: Three Generative Energies of Poetry*.

She has also published two collections of essays, *Nine Gates: Entering the Mind of Poetry*, (HarperCollins, 1997) and *Ten Windows: How Great Poems Transform the World* (Knopf, 2015), and has edited and served as co-translator for several acclaimed and much reprinted volumes collecting the work of women poets of the past: *The Ink Dark Moon: Love Poems by Ono no Komachi and Izumi Shikibu, Women of the Ancient Court of Japan* (Scribner's, 1988; Vintage Classics, 1990); *Women in Praise of the Sacred: 43 Centuries of Spiritual Poetry by Women* (HarperCollins, 1994); and *Mirabai: Ecstatic Poems* (Beacon Press, 2004). Her own poetry has been translated into Polish by Czesław Miłosz (among others), who also wrote the introduction for her bestselling Polish Selected Poems, published by Znak in 2002.

She has taught at the University of California, Berkeley, at Stanford University and elsewhere, and has held many residencies. She has had fellowships from the Guggenheim and Rockefeller foundations, the National Endowment for the Arts, and the Academy of American Poets. In 2012 she was elected a Chancellor of the Academy of American Poets, and in 2019 she was inducted into the American Academy of Arts and Sciences.

JANE HIRSHFIELD

Ledger

BLOODAXE BOOKS

ISBN: 978 1 78037 512 0

First published in the UK in 2020 by
Bloodaxe Books Ltd,
Eastburn,
South Park,
Hexham,
Northumberland NE46 1BS,

and in the US by Alfred A. Knopf, Inc.

www.bloodaxebooks.com
For further information about Bloodaxe titles
please visit our website and join our mailing list
or write to the above address for a catalogue

Supported using public funding by
**ARTS COUNCIL
ENGLAND**

Cover design: Neil Astley & Pamela Robertson-Pearce.

Printed in Great Britain by Bell & Bain Limited, Glasgow, Scotland, on
acid-free paper sourced from mills with FSC chain of custody certification.

CONTENTS

11   Let Them Not Say

     *

15   The Bowl
16   I wanted to be surprised.
18   Vest
20   An Archaeology
21   *Fecit*
22   Day Beginning with Seeing the International Space Station
     and a Full Moon over the Gulf of Mexico and All Its
     Invisible Fishes
23   As If Hearing Heavy Furniture Moved on the Floor
     Above Us
24   Description
25   Ants' Nest
26   A Bucket Forgets Its Water
27   Questionnaire
29   You Go to Sleep in One Room and Wake in Another
30   Chance darkened me.
31   Some Questions
33   Today, Another Universe
34   The Orphan Beauty of Fold Not Made Blindfold

     *

37   Now a Darkness Is Coming
38   Words
39   Homs
40   She Breathes in the Scent
41   A Folding Screen
42   Practice
43   Cataclysm

44   Paint

45   Heels

46   Cold, Clear

47   Capital: An Assay

49   Falcon

50   Spell to Be Said Against Hatred

*

53   Advice to Myself

54   Notebook

55   In Ulvik

56   O Snail

57   Branch

58   Without Night-shoes

59   The Bird Net

60   Corals, Coho, Coelenterates

61   To My Fifties

62   Brocade

63   Interruption: An Assay

65   My Doubt

67   My Contentment

68   My Hunger

69   My Longing

70   My Dignity

72   My Glasses

73   My Wonder

74   My Silence

*

77   A Ream of Paper

78   Lure

79   A Moment Knows Itself Penultimate

81   Bluefish

82   Almond, Rabbit

83   The Paw-paw
84   Musa Paradisiaca
85   It Was as if a Ladder
87   Like Others
88   Husband
89   Wild Turkeys
90   Nine Pebbles
90   WITHOUT BLINKING
90   LIKE THAT OTHER-HAND MUSIC
90   RETROSPECTIVE
91   LIBRARY BOOK WITH MANY PRECISELY TURNED-DOWN CORNERS
91   NOW EVEN MORE
91   HAIKU: MONADNOCK
92   A STRATEGY
92   SIXTH EXTINCTION
92   OBSTACLE
93   They Have Decided
94   Things Seem Strong
95   Dog Tag
96   Biophilia

         *

99   Amor Fati
100   Snow
101   Kitchen
102   Harness
103   Rust Flakes on Wind
104   Pelt
105   Wood. Salt. Tin.
106   I Said

         *

109   Ledger

110   In a Former Coal Mine in Silesia

111   Engraving: World-tree with an Empty Beehive on One Branch

112   (No Wind, No Rain)

113   On the Fifth Day

115   Page

117   My Confession

118   Ghazal for the End of Time

119   Mountainal

120   My Debt

125   ACKNOWLEDGEMENTS

LEDGER

Let Them Not Say

Let them not say: we did not see it.
We saw.

Let them not say: we did not hear it.
We heard.

Let them not say: they did not taste it.
We ate, we trembled.

Let them not say: it was not spoken, not written.
We spoke,
we witnessed with voices and hands.

Let them not say: they did nothing.
We did not-enough.

Let them say, as they must say something:

A kerosene beauty.
It burned.

Let them say we warmed ourselves by it,
read by its light, praised,
and it burned.

The Bowl

If meat is put into the bowl, meat is eaten.

If rice is put into the bowl, it may be cooked.

If a shoe is put into the bowl,
the leather is chewed and chewed over,
a sentence that cannot be taken in or forgotten.

A day, if a day could feel, must feel like a bowl.
Wars, loves, trucks, betrayals, kindness,
it eats them.

Then the next day comes, spotless and hungry.

The bowl cannot be thrown away.
It cannot be broken.

It is calm, uneclipsable, rindless,
and, big though it seems, fits exactly in two human hands.

Hands with ten fingers,
fifty-four bones,
capacities strange to us almost past measure.
Scented—as the curve of the bowl is—
with cardamom, star anise, long pepper, cinnamon, hyssop.

I wanted to be surprised.

To such a request, the world is obliging.

In just the past week, a rotund porcupine,
who seemed equally startled by me.

The man who swallowed a tiny microphone
to record the sounds of his body,
not considering beforehand how he might remove it.

A cabbage and mustard sandwich on marbled bread.

How easily the large spiders were caught with a clear plastic cup
surprised even them.

I don't know why I was surprised every time love started or ended.
Or why each time a new fossil, Earth-like planet, or war.
Or that no one kept being there when the doorknob had clearly.

What should not have been so surprising:
my error after error, recognised when appearing on the faces of others.

What did not surprise enough:
my daily expectation that anything would continue,
and then that so much did continue, when so much did not.

Small rivulets still flowing downhill when it wasn't raining.
A sister's birthday.

Also, the stubborn, courteous persistence.
That even today *please* means *please*,
good morning is still understood as *good morning*,

and that when I wake up,
the window's distant mountain remains a mountain,
the borrowed city around me is still a city, and standing.

Its alleys and markets, offices of dentists,
drug store, liquor store, Chevron.
Its library that charges – a happy surprise – no fine for overdue books:
Borges, Baldwin, Szymborska, Morrison, Cavafy.

Vest

I put on again the vest of many pockets.

It is easy to forget
which holds the reading glasses,
which the small pen,
which the house keys,
the compass and whistle, the passport.

To forget at last for weeks
even the pocket holding the day
of digging a place for my sister's ashes,
the one holding the day
where someone will soon enough put my own.

To misplace the pocket
of touching the walls at Auschwitz
would seem impossible.
It is not.

To misplace, for a decade,
the pocket of tears.

I rummage and rummage—
transfers
for Munich, for Melbourne,
to Oslo.
A receipt for a Singapore *kopi*.
A device holding music:
Bach, Garcia, Richter, Porter, Pärt.

A woman long dead now
gave me, when I told her I could not sing,
a kazoo.
Now in a pocket.

Somewhere, a pocket
holding a Steinway.
Somewhere, a pocket
holding a packet of salt.

Borgesian vest,
Oxford English Dictionary vest
with a magnifying glass
tucked inside one snapped-closed pocket,
Wikipedia vest, Rosetta vest,
Enigma vest of decoding,
how is it one person can carry
your weight for a lifetime,
one person
slip into your open arms for a lifetime?

Who was given the world,
and hunted for tissues, for chapstick.

An Archaeology

Sixty feet below the streets of Rome,
the streets of Rome.
Like that, I heard your voice, my life.
Like that I listened.

I listened
as to neighbors who live
behind the back wall of a building.

You know the voices of them,
the arguments and re-knittings,
the scents of their cooking and absence.
You know their plosives, gutturals, fricatives, stops.

Say to any who walk here,
'How are you?'
Ask where some bar or café might be found.
You could talk together, and drink,
and find your own neighbor.

But ask your life anything, ask it,
'How did this happen? What have we come to?'
It turns its face, it hums as a fish-hiding sea does.

Fecit

for a person in love, the air looks no different

for a person in grief

in this my one lifetime,
while reading, arguing, cherishing, washing, watching a video,
sleeping,
the numbers unseeably rise—

305 ppm, 317 ppm, 390, 400

shin of high granite ticks snow-less the compound fracture

I who wrote this

like the old painters
sign this:

JH fecit.

Day Beginning with Seeing the International Space Station and a Full Moon over the Gulf of Mexico and All Its Invisible Fishes

None of this had to happen.
Not Florida. Not the ibis's beak. Not water.
Not the horseshoe crab's empty body and not the living starfish.
Evolution might have turned left at the corner and gone down another
    street entirely.
The asteroid might have missed.
The seams of limestone need not have been susceptible to sand and
    mangroves.
The radio might have found a different music.
The hips of one man and the hips of another might have stood beside
each other on a bus in Aleppo and recognised themselves as long-lost
    brothers.
The key could have broken off in the lock and the nail-can refused its
    lid.
I might have been the fish the brown pelican swallowed.
You might have been the way the moon kept not setting long after we
    thought it would,
long after the sun was catching inside the low wave curls coming in
at a certain angle. The light might not have been eaten again by its
    moving.
If the unbearable were not weightless we might yet buckle under the
    grief
of what hasn't changed yet. Across the world a man pulls a woman
    from the water
from which the leapt-from overfilled boat has entirely vanished.
From the water pulls one child, another. Both are living and both will
    continue to live.
This did not have to happen. No part of this had to happen.

As If Hearing Heavy Furniture Moved on the Floor Above Us

As things grow rarer, they enter the ranges of counting.
Remain this many Siberian tigers,
that many African elephants. Three hundred red-legged egrets.
We scrape from the world its tilt and meander of wonder
as if eating the last burned onions and carrots from a cast-iron pan.
Closing eyes to taste better the char of ordinary sweetness.

Description

Humans: beings directional,
symmetrical.

With left and right hands,
left and right feet,
ears that hear lullabies
from one side or the other,
nostrils that know fear or food
from one side or the other.

Beings who sneeze
while following a trail
through wet woods
to whose asters and mosses
two eyes bring stereoscopic depth.

Sometimes, it's true, the ears mishear:
death.

Sometimes the feet's direction is only away.

Sometimes the hands misunderstand their task.
They tremble.
They ask their wrists: *This?*

Fingers with such sensitive nerve ends,
such solicitude holding a chisel or cello,
they thought they were meant to inflict only beauty and kindness.

Ants' Nest

'On Being the Right Size', Haldane's short essay is titled.

An ants' nest can be found at the top of a redwood.

No bird that weighs less than _____.
No insect more than _____.
The minimum mass for a whale, for a language, an ice cap.

In a human-sized room,
someone is setting a human-sized table with yellow napkins,
someone is calling
her children to come in from a day whose losses as yet remain
child-sized.

A Bucket Forgets Its Water

A bucket forgets its water,
its milk, its paint.
Washed out, re-used, it can be washed again.

I admire the amnesia of buckets.

How they are forthright and infinite inside it,
simple of purpose,
how their single seam is as thin of rib as a donkey's.

A bucket upside down
is almost as useful as upright—
step stool, tool shelf, drum stand, small table for lunch.

A bucket receives and returns all it is given,
holds no grudges, fears,
or regret.

A bucket striking the mop sink rings clearest when empty.

But not one can bray.

Questionnaire

Oddly, I liked them,
liked answering,
as I liked to look
at a tree or a mountain
and hear their own questions,
undistracted and steady.
As I liked to look at a horse
who would sometimes look back.

Each was a small emergency,
a requiring.

Pressing, we say:
a pressing question.

As if something were oil within us
that could be released
and then cooked with,
as if something in us could be lit
and set bowl-held to burn,
its yellow light going one way,
its scent another.

As one by one
did the questions,
along with their schoolrooms,
hospitals, offices for hiring—
tests forced and tests chosen,
tests minor, tests idle,
tests factual or subjective,
taking with them
the filled-in and empty bubbles,

the provisional guesses,
the clear-as-day answers,
taking with them
the right, the wrong, the ink,
the pen, my own unanswerable life.

You Go to Sleep in One Room and Wake in Another

You go to sleep in one room and wake in another.
You go to sleep in one time and wake in another.

Men land on the moon!—
Viewed in blurred black and white, in static,
on a big screen in Central Park, standing in darkness with others.

Your grandfather did not see this.
Your grandchildren will not see this.
Soon now, fifty years back.

Unemphatic, the wheelbarrowed stars hung above.

Many days, like a nephew,
resemble the one beforehand,
but they are not the one beforehand.
Each was singular, spendable, eaten with pepper and salt.

You go to sleep in one person's bed and wake in another's,
your face after toweling changed from the face that was washed.

You go to sleep in one world and wake in another.

You who were not your life nor were stranger to it,
you who were not
your name, your ribs, your skin,
will go as a suitcase that takes inside it the room—

Only after you know this can you know this.
As a knocked glass that loses what has been spilled, you will know
    this.

Chance darkened me.

Chance darkened me

as a morning darkens,
preparing to rain.

It goes against its arc,
betrays its clock-hands.

The day was a dark-eyed giraffe,
its unfathomable legs
kept walking.

A person is not a day,
not rain,
no gentle eater of high leaves.

I did not keep walking.
The day inside me,
legs and lungs, kept walking.

Some Questions

Who first asked it?
The sand or the footprint,
the remembering or the forgetting?

*

A house, a door, an hour—
which is frame, which picture?

*

Where found, old grief-joy,
your salvage-yard windows and shutters,
your emergency, your emergence?

*

Me, you / us, them—
What
molecule   cell   creature
came first to feel it?

*

Was it painful?

*

How came separation to chisel,
to cherish, to chafe?

*

Hammock of burning carbon
life wove from,
hammock life slept in,
unraveling—

did you find us useful,
interesting,
comic?

*

Will you miss them,
the cruelty and hunger,
the manatees and spoonbills,

awe's inexplicable swaying?

Today, Another Universe

The arborist has determined:
senescence   beetles   canker
quickened by drought
                but in any case
not prunable   not treatable   not to be propped.

And so.

The branch from which the sharp-shinned hawks and their mate-cries.

The trunk where the ant.

The red squirrels' eighty-foot playground.

The bark   cambium   pine-sap   cluster of needles.

The Japanese patterns   the ink-net.

The dapple on certain fish.

Today, for some, a universe will vanish.
First noisily,
then just another silence.

The silence of *after*, once the theater has emptied.

Of bewilderment after the glacier,
the species, the star.

Something else, in the scale of quickening things,
will replace it,

this hole of light in the light, the puzzled birds swerving around it.

The Orphan Beauty of Fold Not Made Blindfold

A house seems solid, and yet, in the living, any footstep shakes it.

As if walking in wind toward de Kooning's late paintings,
whose brush had been tied to his hand.

'I sing not for the music,
I sing to keep the bitterness from the sorrow,'
hum the words of a *cante jondo*, far from their home.

A thought comes to your bed in the night.
You accept, take it blindly, by darkness,
                                as you once did a love—
feeling the bed starting to tremble before it was entered.

Not knowing whose the wanting, whose the beauty,
but wanting that wanting.

The salt shine and

blundering toward it. Blundering and blundering toward it.

Now a Darkness Is Coming

I hold my life with two hands.
I walk with two legs.
Two ears are enough to hear Bach with.

Blinded in one eye, a person sees with the other.

Now a great darkness is coming.
A both-eyes darkness.

I have one mouth.
It holds two words.
Yes, No,
inside all others.

Yes. No. No. Yes.

I say yes to these words, as I must,
and I also refuse them.

My two legs,
shaped to go forward,
obedient to can't-know and must-be,
walk into the time that is coming.

Words

Words are loyal.
Whatever they name they take the side of.
As the word *courage* will afterward grip just as well
the frightened girl soldier who stands on one side of barbed wire,
the frightened boy soldier who stands on the other.
Death's clay, they look at each other with wide-open eyes.
And words—that love peace, love gossip—refuse to condemn them.

Homs

Wind this morning
so strong the borrowed Florida house shakes
on its stilts over water.

White pelicans, which do not resemble the spirit,
write their single sentence
straight through it, unhindered.
Their rowing wings dipped long ago into some inkpot.

Rapacity doesn't swerve before what it feasts on.

To a not-fish, a bird is beauty.
To a not-fish, hunger
wrings out its morning swim-towel and re-hangs it.

Yesterday's Russian-drone-taken video,
watched on computer:
window after window, glassless, glintless.

Apartment blocks, streetlights, market squares
past-plunged, deafened, unstoried.

Three incomprehensible men
look up,
wave at the camera from inside their shirts' bright colors.

Around them, the no-longer city.
Its no-longer purses and breasts, esophagi, cellphones, slippers, suppers.

No fish-teeming world nor its spiraling wings can redeem this.

(No feather, shell, word, image redeem this.)

She Breathes in the Scent

As the front of a box would miss the sides,
the back,

the grief of the living
misses the grief of the dead.

It is
like a woman who goes to the airport
to meet the planes from a country she long ago lived in.

She knows no passenger but stands near as they exit
still holding their passports.

She breathes in the scent of their clothes.

A Folding Screen

The news keeps coming,
         with its one crooked
finger.

     death   death   death   death   death

And one no longer turns at the call of her name,
and another forgets to lift his surprised eyebrow.

While here the ducklings,
          and the duckling descendants,
      cross the squares of the centuries' gold-leafed painting,
as if inside the crease of a still living river.

Practice

I touch my toes.

When I was a child,
this was difficult.
Now I touch my toes daily.

In 2012, in Sanford, Florida,
someone nearby was touching her toes before bed.

Three weeks ago,
in the Philippines or Myanmar, someone was stretching.

Tomorrow, someone elsewhere will bend
first to one side, then the other.

I also do ten push-ups, morning and evening.

Women's push-ups,
from the knees.
They resemble certain forms of religious bowing.

In place of *one, two, four, seven,*
I count the names of incomprehension: *Sanford, Ferguson, Charleston.*
Aleppo, Sarajevo, Nagasaki.

I never reach: *Troy, Ur.*

I have done this for years now.
Bystander. Listener. One of the lucky.
I do not seem to grow stronger.

Cataclysm

It begins subtly:
the maple
withdraws an inch from the birch tree.

The porcupine
wants nothing to do with the skink.

Fish unschool,
sheep unflock to separately graze.

Clouds meanwhile
declare to the sky
they have nothing to do with the sky,
which is not visible as they are,

nor knows the trick of turning
into infant, tumbling pterodactyls.

The turtles and moonlight?
Their long arrangement is over.

As for the humans.
Let us not speak of the humans.
Let us speak of their language.

The first-person singular
condemns the second-person plural
for betrayals neither has words left to name.

The fed consider the hungry
and stay silent.

Paint

Someone invented this.

If a person
pees on a wall so painted,
the pee splashes back,
wets the pants, soaks the shoes.

Surprise! the wall says.

Someone thought this a good solution.
Someone gave it a color.

Heels

Thump. Thump. Thump.
I am back in my childhood apartment.
Thump.
Someone above is sleepless, again.
Thump, thump.
I agree:
I, too, am now awake, sleepless.
How uncomfortably we went on together,
intimate and unmarried:
16A, 15A.
Sometimes a different sound,
a jar of spilled marbles.
More often: thump.
Shared nights
that seemed then forever.
Though tonight it is only me.
My own frightened heartbeat,
my own once-childhood country.

Cold, Clear

A person
dreams herself blind
hearing the click of a light switch.

*

Forty years since the wake-up *han*'s
much battered ink-written
'Don't waste time.'

*

Night-weather's hearable.

Sometimes the mallet-sound sharp,
other times muffled.

*

Self, too, was hearable inside and outside
the

skin
inside and outside the scent of creek and pine.

*

Stars, wind, day, night, pine bark.
They don't need us.

They don't need to be stars, wind, day, night, pine bark.

Capital: An Assay

In the 1925 edition of *Roget's Thesaurus*, the first listing for 'capital' appears, unsurprisingly, under the category of 'money'. Among the list of synonyms, not very far down: *rhino, blunt, dust, mopus, tin, salt, chink*. Higher up: *sinews of war, almighty dollar, needful*. Lower: *wampum, lac of rupees, plum*. The word's second-place index listing sends the reader to 'wealth'. There you can find among its companion concepts: *El Dorado, Pactolus, Golconda, Potosi*; also the more easily comprehended but equally culturally dependent alimony and dowry.

The Pactolus, further research reveals, is a Turkish river near the Aegean coast. Its sediments contain electrum, a naturally occurring alloy of silver and gold. Electrum from the Pactolus underlay the economy of the ancient state of Lydia, the first Western imperium to issue coins and open shops. Electrum mixed – debased – with copper was known as 'green gold'. According to myth, King Midas first deposited the riverbed's stores of precious metals when he washed in the Pactolus to undo his curse. King Croesus's legendary riches, according to Herodotus, were drawn from its waters. A photograph shows a pretty, greenish river passing between scenic white rocks.

In the midst of these readings, I find myself pausing to eat a small, flat peach of perfect color and ripeness. Gone in a few quick bites, in what is likely the last possible hour it will be good.

Though a peach's ripeness will always elude 'Possessive Relations' – the larger category in which all words related to capital appear – I take my pencil and add to the *Thesaurus*: *peach*. Surely no less incomprehensible to someone in the future than *rhino*, *blunt*, and *dust* are now to me. I write it not next to *plum*, but where there's a bit of extra space: right after the entry *loaves and fishes*, at the end of a list that begins *pelf*, *Mammon, lucre, filthy lucre*.

The presence of *plum* is explained – somewhat – in a dictionary of slang: *A desirable thing. A raisin, when used in a pudding or cake. (pejorative) A fool, idiot. (slang, usually in plural) A testicle. The edible, fleshy stone fruit of Prunus mume, an Asian fruit more closely related to the apricot than the plum, usually consumed pickled, dried, or as a juice or wine; ume.* I am oddly delighted to find that last, Japanese word in the entry.

A writer's capital is language, which, it seems, is as slippery as any other kind of wealth, as potentially cursed if held without nuance, as transient, as bluntly and inextricably subjective. A briefly borrowed inheritance; a street-found penny. In another ninety years, I can't help but wonder, will penny be a word so unfamiliar it too will need looking up, another *mopus*? Yet to be penniless will be just as painful when named in some other way.

Falcon

Incapable of betrayal: a tree.

Incapable of holding a secret: a stone.

Without contempt for self or other:
an ant, a bee.

Today I and the unhooded bird
that sits on my head
are looking in different directions,
I into the blurring past, he into the blurring future.

How many other pasts and futures,
between and around us, we miss.

Incapable of ungenerosity: grass;
cut, it simply keeps growing.

Without obligation: mosquitoes.

How close to human
must the breathed-in air come
before it develops a sense of shame or humor?

Each day the falcon's view a little clearer.

Spell to Be Said Against Hatred

Until each breath refuses *they*, *those*, *them*.
Until the *Dramatis Personae* of the book's first page says, 'Each one is you.'
Until hope bows to its hopelessness only as one self bows to another.
Until cruelty bends to its work and sees suddenly: *I*.
Until anger and insult know themselves burnable legs of a useless table.
Until the unsurprised unbidden knees find themselves bending.
Until fear bows to its object as a bird's shadow bows to its bird.
Until the ache of the solitude inside the hands, the ribs, the ankles.
Until the sound the mouse makes inside the mouth of the cat.
Until the inaudible acids bathing the coral.
Until what feels no one's weighing is no longer weightless.
Until what feels no one's earning is no longer taken.
Until grief, pity, confusion, laughter, longing know themselves mirrors.
Until by *we* we mean I, them, you, the muskrat, the tiger, the hunger.
Until by *I* we mean as a dog barks, sounding and vanishing and
    sounding and vanishing completely.
Until by *until* we mean I, we, you, them, the muskrat, the tiger, the
    hunger, the lonely barking of the dog before it is answered.

Advice to Myself

The computer file
of which
I have no recollection
is labeled 'advice to myself'

I click it open
look
scroll further down

the screen
stays backlit and empty

thus I meet myself again
hopeful and useless

a mystery

precisely as I must
have done
on August 19, 2010, 11:08 A.M.

Notebook

A Venus flytrap can count to five.
Crows and bees recognise faces.
Mice suffer when seeing a mouse who is known to them suffer.
Trees warn one another to alter their sap as beetles draw near.

Our one remaining human distinction:
a pre-Copernican pride in our human distinction.

'Arthritis in both ankles!'
Neruda wrote in a notebook,
January 3, 1959, on a boat leaving Valparaíso for Venezuela,

limping like an old racehorse, then starting his poem.

In Ulvik

He spent his whole life in Ulvik, working as a gardener in his own orchard.

(OF OLAV HAUGE)

I, too, would like to work
as a gardener in my own orchard.
Every Friday I would pay myself
a decent, living wage,
taken in foldable cash from my own wallet,
and sometimes, if the weather was bad,
I would give myself the day off
and thank myself for my kindness
and answer myself, It's nothing, nothing, go on now,
put your feet up, find somewhere warm.
And then I would go back into my house
and think of my kindness
and wonder if my gardener was warm now also
and if I was right to let myself
go away from my own orchard's tending
even so briefly, and each of us
might be thinking, too, of the apples,
cold and wet and hanging in outside wind
and fattening on their own trees without us,
and one of us, first, then the other,
might start to wonder a little,
while pushing a cut of cured applewood into the fire,
about loneliness and separateness and what
it is lives outside one person's skin and inside another's.

O Snail

Under the Svalbard ice cap, Carboniferous-era coal seams.
A good farmer rotates her crops.
The crops don't complain. It's the fate of stalks and forests to vanish.
Last year's fires: Australia, Portugal, Greece. This: California.

O snail, wrote Issa, climb Fuji slowly, slowly.

Branch

A clock does not have hands, a face,
tell anything, rightly or wrongly, least of all time.

An empty branch does not long for its nondescript bird.

The bird is not the quick dash
that holds separate the world's *Yes* from the world's *No*.

Is there anywhere on earth one branch that has never been perched on?

That is not what branches exist for. Yet the birds come.

Without Night-shoes

All night,
sonatas played left-handed,
inside a loaned iPod.

Neither sleeping nor waking,
I walked their unshod stairways,
up and then down.

On some blackboard inside the house,
the word *fear*
vanished.

On some blackboard inside the house,
the word *far* vanished.

Then the word *error*, then *or*.

Grave and slender,
those hours unhoured themselves,
stair by stair vanished.

C minor, E flat, F sharp, A sharp erased them.

The Bird Net

I once decided to pretend to be angry.

Then I was.

As a bird is caught in its birdness before it is caught in the bird net.

The bird might be counted, tagged, released.
The bird might be eaten.

It took hours for the shaking to leave my body.

Body of air, body of branch, what earth's yellows & nectars were
    made for.

Corals, Coho, Coelenterates

I keep a white page before me.
Each time one
is marred with effort, striving, effect, I turn to another.

Corals, coho, coelenterates
inside the waving arms of your branches
that give off a scent intoxicant only to certain fish—

lichens, burdocks, mycelial mats between trees—
forgive this hubris.
                Some hope is in it.
Your companions are new here.

A child who crayons does not know
her drawing leaves behind absence on forest, on ocean.

She falls into the colors.

To My Fifties

You opened me
as a burglar opens a house with a silent alarm.
I opened you
as a burglar opens a house with a silent alarm.

We knew we had to work quickly,
bears ecstatic, not minding the stinging.

Or say it was this:

We were the wax paper bag
in which something was wrapped.
What was inside us
neither opaque nor entirely transparent.
Afterward, we were folded into neat creases.

Or this:

Say we were paired
parentheses
cupping two dates, a hyphen,
and much that continues unspoken.

Say:

We were our own future,
a furnace invented to burn itself up.

Brocade

All day wondering
if I've become useless.

All day the osprey
white and black,
carrying
big dry sticks without leaves.

Late, I said to my pride,

You think you're the feathered part
of this, do you?

Interruption: An Assay

Sometimes you took the shape
of an unseen mosquito,
sometimes of illness.

Presumed most of the time to be passing,
yet importunate as a toddler
who demanded her own way,
as a phone that would not stop ringing long after it should.

Unignorable pavement slap of the gone-flat tire.

All afternoon the thunder was interrupted by sunshine.
All night the rain was interrupted by trees and roofs.

And still, as rusting steel is uninterrupted by dryness
and hunger uninterrupted by sleep,
interruption and non-interruption sat in the day's container
as salt sits in milk, one whiteness disguised by another.

As a fish in a tank is interrupted by glass, and turns,
a person's fate is to continue
despite,
until.

Death: an interruption not passing,
weighing
one hundred and fifty-eight pounds,
carried on cut plywood with yellow straps.

Birth: an interruption between
two windows,
trying to think of any joke, any tune, that is new.

Between them:
this navigation by echolocation and lidar,
the weathers of avalanche, earthquake, tsunami,
firestorm, drought;
a moment that sets down – gently, sleepily – its half-read novel
on a bedside table whose side turned toward the wall stays unpainted,
confident the story will be there again come morning.

My Doubt

I wake, doubt, beside you,
like a curtain half-open.

I dress doubting,
like a cup
undecided if it has been dropped.

I eat doubting,
work doubting,
go out to a dubious café with skeptical friends.

I go to sleep doubting myself,
as a herd of goats
sleep in a suddenly gone-quiet truck.

I dream you, doubt,
nightly—
for what is the meaning of dreaming
if not that all we are while inside it
is transient, amorphous, in question?

Left hand and right hand,
doubt, you are in me,
throwing a basketball, guiding my knife and my fork.
Left knee and right knee,
we run for a bus,
for a meeting that surely will end before we arrive.

I would like
to grow content in you, doubt,
as a double-hung window
settles obedient into its hidden pulleys and ropes.

I doubt I can do so:
your own counterweight governs my nights and my days.

As the knob of hung lead holds steady
the open mouth of a window,
you hold me,
my kneeling before you resistant, stubborn,
offering these furious praises
I can't help but doubt you will ever be able to hear.

My Contentment

I reject contentment:
into it, certain inexperienced saints have been seen to vanish,
in a burst of somewhat cloudy light.

My Hunger

The way the high-wire walker
must carry a pole
to make her arms longer

you carried me   I carried you
through this world.

My Longing

My hope, my despair, my longing.

Every pocket I put you in had its hole.
Mouse and moth, too, have their hungers.

I called you my life.

Good dog, I said, good dog, as if we could answer.

My Dignity

My dignity drinks with me
a cup of coffee, with sugar and milk,
in a bathrobe.

My dignity, this day,
neither adds to nor subtracts from
the dignity of any other.

My dignity, this one day,
closes its ledgers.

Its luxury, this day, is coffee, sugar, and milk.
Is having enough to want nothing.

Soon my dignity,
unwitnessed, unwitnessing,
will dress
in clothes no one will judge for their wrinkles,
in skin no one will judge for its fit.

My dignity, I know,
could be taken from me easily,
invisibly, in a single pickpocketed instant.
An errant driver. An errant rock. An errant anger.

My own heart could take it—
one moment, drinking coffee,
the next—

My own breast or marrow could take it.

But my dignity and I do not apologise
to one another,
this day,
nor, this day, profess to more than we can.

I know I will someday say to my dignity:
It's all right, I know it is time,
leave if you must, live elsewhere.

Take with you, like a good sous-chef,
your towel-wrapped knife and whetstone,
your luck-bringing ladle.

My Glasses

Glasses can be taken off.
The world instantly softens, blurs.
The pattern of carpet
or leaves out a window,
words on a page,
the face in a mirror.
Blurs,
even the war that is coming,
pushing its iron boat-shape
onto the sand of a beach not far
but not seen;
even the silences coming,
following the boat
as a swimming dog follows its master.
Lu Chi, poet and scholar,
born into a family of generals,
was executed
in the thirty-fifth year of the Xī Jin dynasty,
after his soldiers' bodies
blocked the Great Yangtze.
The Yangtze went elsewhere,
blurring the nearby fields.
Merciful blurring, merciful forgetting.
Meeting Lu Chi's name.
I think of his image of culture
as one axe handle shaping another,
I think of his thought about unpainted silk.
Each of the Yangtze dead
had a mother, a father, wife, children,
a well, some chickens.
No, the largesse of glasses is not seeing.

My Wonder

That it is one-half degree centigrade.
That I eat honeydew melon
for breakfast.
That I look out through the oval window.
That I am able to look out through an oval window.

My Silence

A Ream of Paper

I have a ream of paper,
a cartridge of ink,

almonds,
coffee,
a wool scarf for warmth.

Whatever handcuffs the soul,
I have brought here.

Whatever distances the heart,
I have brought here.

A deer rises onto her haunches
to reach for an apple,

though many fallen apples are on the ground.

Lure

I waited though wanting nothing,
then waited longer.

As if by that I might
become again
the carved and painted lure—

Its two iridescent eyes that stay always open,
its stippled gold sides, deep orange back,
red threads attached at the gills.

I hummed with its three-pronged shine
of fish who are sweet and fat to the birds above them.

I hummed with its three injured notes to the fish below.

To all the blue-winged, handless distances
and all my blue-finned, handless lives,
I hummed
in borrowed Swedish and the iron-hiding slip of gleam—

The great strangeness still may come, even for you.

A Moment Knows Itself Penultimate

A moment knows itself penultimate—
usable, spendable,
good yet, but only for reckoning up.

A moment knows something's almost over,
but not what it is.

There is still time, the day sings its old round, time still is here,
though you can't hear
the new thing arriving inside the knots of its ticking,

though you can't feel the brush of its wing
on the nape of your life,

or hope for the voice
to arrive, as it has always, saying,
'Come, I've returned to you, here is your gift.'

The moment finds itself weary,
blindered,
language confuses its ears.

Some things that are frayed
can be
turned inside out, can be darned, can be quilted.

Others are used up completely.

It's like the custom for the widow at certain funerals—

Friends speak,
children,
the many and long-disguised lovers.

The widow's task is different.
She does not speak.

Bluefish

We once threw
empty soda cans out bus windows,
thoughtless
as all of our kind.

Mice, rabbits.

That changed.
The highways grew prettier.

On one coast, we ate Oregon forests.
On the other, cod banks and bluefish.

Teethed, we were.
Handed.
Mammals needing to nap,
to leap a little when happy or frightened.

Almond, Rabbit

Each thing you eat,
another future disappears from the future.

Its nests,
its lichens, thirsts, fleas, spiders.

And if you yourself now were eaten,
you would taste of almond or rabbit,
not future.

Some futures you might have liked more,
some less.

Birds enter and leave them elsewhere.

The Paw-paw

A woman speaks to me
of a paw-paw tree.

I have never seen a paw-paw tree.
I have never eaten its fruit.

I nod.
The conversation continues.

So many things
we think we understand,
until we stop to think.

Her life.

My own.

Musa Paradisiaca

Outside the window
big eight-foot leaves
lift taller
than the height of the island they rise from.

Green faces unmoving,
rain runs down and outside their nearness.

— *else   there   when* —

Such thoughts do not touch them.

The rain does not touch them.
They stand.

Only I at a night window,
thinking,
as if from inside the hull of a handmade boat:

Though it is not words that turn you,
chlorophyll sorrow,
do not abandon here your faithless servants.

It Was as if a Ladder

It was as if
a ladder,

and each rung,
real to itself,
round or slat,
narrow or wide,
rope or metal—

and as you ascended,
real to yourself,
the rungs directly above
you solid,
directly beneath you, solid.

Scent of peeled orange
mixed with gasoline,
sound of hammers.

Farther below,
the rungs one by one vanished.

Farther above,
the rungs one by one
vanished.

And the side rails' lines
vanished, as into
a drawing by Brunelleschi.

Scent of peeled orange
and gasoline,
sound of hammers.

Grip now, night-dog, your barking:

this ladder in air,
invented by others, received by others.

Like Others

In the end,
I was like others.
A person.

Sometimes embarrassed,
sometimes afraid.

When 'Fire!' was shouted,
some ran toward it,
some away—

I neck-deep among them.

Husband

Some things can surprise you in both directions,
coming and going.

Like a stretch of single train track with shuntings over.

The auto-correct I don't know how to stop
suggested, just now, 'overwhelming',
with shuntings overwhelming. Almost I took that.

Almost I took you as husband, love. Then you left me.

I took surprise for husband instead.

The Phoenician letter for 'h', pronounced *heth*,
resembled at first
a slanting, three-runged ladder.
Later it straightened, becoming a double-hung window.

Husband surprise, I climbed you, I climbed right out you.

Wild Turkeys

Two remnant-dinosaur wild turkeys
walk between silence and silence. Not to themselves a meal of meat.
I, who am to myself also not meat, feed mosquitoes nightly,
though day and night I wait for hunger
to find me its dark wood violin, inside its dark wood case.

Nine Pebbles

WITHOUT BLINKING

House a little cold, stomach a little hungry,
hands a little empty.

The planet is porous, wrote Borges, and so it might be claimed
that all men have bathed in the holy Ganges.

Sponges alone,
that live always filled, may filter this thought without blinking.

LIKE THAT OTHER-HAND MUSIC

Like that other-hand
music
written for one who has lost an arm in a war,
you, hope, may again become useful.

RETROSPECTIVE

No photograph or painting can hold it—
the stillness of water
just before it starts being ice.

LIBRARY BOOK WITH MANY PRECISELY TURNED-DOWN CORNERS

I unfold carefully the thoughts of one who has come before me,
the way a listening dog's ears
may be seen lifting
to some sound beyond its person's quite understanding.

NOW EVEN MORE

Now again, even more, I admire Roget,
in whose *Thesaurus*
self-knowledge appears under *Modesty*.

Following *verecundity* – knowing one's place;
preceding *reserve*.

HAIKU: MONADNOCK

November rain—
two bronze deer turn to face me
as I pass.

A STRATEGY

Continuing by implication.
Anywhere the ink isn't is moon.

SIXTH EXTINCTION

It took with it
the words that could have described it.

OBSTACLE

This body, still walking.
The wind must go around it.

They Have Decided

Comes a time they have decided who you are.
But you have not decided who you are.

Your wrists have decided.
Your knees have decided.
The hair that will leave its braidings behind has decided.

Your ears, your rebelling ears,
have decided: enough.
They surrender cities, pianos, sentences, whistlings, cries.

Your thoughts, it seemed once, had decided.
But you, past naming, past weighing, have not decided.

Like a foal still trying to find which leg goes where for standing:
you have not decided.

Things Seem Strong

Things seem strong.
Houses, trees, trucks—a chair, even.
A table. A country.

You don't expect one to break.
No, it takes a hammer to break one,
a war, a saw, an earthquake.

Troy after Troy after Troy seemed strong
to those living around and in them.
Nine Troys were strong,
each trembling under the other.

When the ground floods
and the fire ants leave their strong city,
they link legs and form a raft, and float, and live,
and begin again elsewhere.

Strong, your life's wish
to continue linking arms with life's eye blink, life's tear well,
life's hammering of copper sheets and planing of Port Orford cedar,
life's joke of the knock-knock.

Knock, knock. Who's there?
I am.
I am who?

That first and last question.

Who once dressed in footed pajamas,
who once was smothered in kisses.
Who seemed so strong
I could not imagine your mouth would ever come to stop asking.

Dog Tag

At last understanding
that everything my friend had been saying
for the thirty-three months since he knew
were words of the dog tag, words of, whatever else,
the milled and stamped-into metal of what stays behind.
Blackcap Mountain. Blue scorpion venom. Persimmon pudding.
He spoke them.
He could not say love enough times.
It clinked against itself, it clinked against its little chain.

Biophilia

Most of us hungry at daybreak, sleepy by dark.
Some slept, one eye open, in water.
Some could trot.
Some of us lived till morning. Some did not.

Amor Fati

Little soul,
you have wandered
lost a long time.

The woods all dark now,
birded and eyed.

Then a light, a cabin, a fire, a door standing open.

The fairy tales warn you:
Do not go in,
you who would eat will be eaten.

You go in. You quicken.

You want to have feet.
You want to have eyes.
You want to have fears.

Snow

Little soul,
for you, too,
death is coming.

Was there something
you thought
you needed to do?

Snow
does not walk into a room

and wonder

why.

Kitchen

Little soul,
how useful was hunger.

From whatever it was we fell into,
you and I,
it sprang open our fingers' grip.

Yet a life is not prepared for its ending
like a sliced eggplant,

salted and pressed to let leave from itself what is bitter.

Harness

Little soul,
you and I will become

the memory
of a memory of a memory.

A horse
released of the traces
forgets the weight of the wagon.

Rust Flakes on Wind

Little soul,
a day comes when retrospection ceases.

A person falling does not, mid-plummet, look up.

Still,
for a few seconds on Wednesday,
'Where are my truck keys?'

On Thursday, on Sunday: 'Where are my truck keys?'

Pelt

Little soul,
the book of your hours
is closing

over its golds,
its reds, your gazing dog,
your rivers, ladders,
rib cage.

A life
turns into its patterns and perfumes,
then into its pelt.

I don't know now
if we were one, if we were two,
a stippling.

Whither thou goest,
we'd said.

Wood. Salt. Tin.

Little soul,
do you remember?

You once walked
over wooden boards
to a house
that sat on stilts in the sea.

It was early.

The sun painted
brightness onto the water,
and wherever you sat
that path
led directly to you.

Some mornings
the sea-road was muted
scratched tin,
some mornings blinding.

Then it would leave.

Little soul,
it is strange—

even now it is early.

I Said

I said   I believed
a world without you unimaginable.

Now cutting its flowers to go with you into the fire.

Ledger

Tchaikovsky's *Eugene Onegin* is 3,592 measures.
A voice kept far from feeling is heard as measured.
What's wanted in desperate times are desperate measures.
Pushkin's unfinished *Onegin*: 5,446 lines.

No visible tears measure the pilot's grief
as she lidars the height of an island: five feet.
Fifty, its highest leaf.
She logs the years, the weathers, the tree has left.

A million fired-clay bones—animal, human—
set down in a field as protest
measure 400 yards long, 60 yards wide, weigh 112 tons.
The length and weight and silence of the bereft.

Bees do not question the sweetness of what sways beneath them.
One measure of distance is meters. Another is *li*.
Ten thousand li can be translated: 'far'.
For the exiled, *home* can be translated 'then', translated 'scar'.

One liter
of Polish vodka holds twelve pounds of potatoes.
What we care about most, we call *beyond measure*.
What matters most, we say *counts*. Height now is treasure.

On this scale of one to ten, where is eleven?
Ask all you wish, no twenty-fifth hour will be given.
Measuring mounts—like some Western bar's mounted elk head—
our catalogued vanishing unfinished heaven.

In a Former Coal Mine in Silesia

In a former coal mine in Silesia, a thousand feet inside the earth,
a tongue kept speaking.

In the Arctic, by the triangular door to the Svalbard seed vault,
a tongue almost fearless, almost not clumsy, spoke.
Spoke verbs, conjunctions, adjectives, adverbs, nouns.

In a small town in the Australian Outback,
in the city of Nanjing, near a gate still recalling unthinkable closures,
by a lake in Montana, a tongue almost steady,
almost not stumbling, spoke facts, hypotheses, memories, riddles, stories.

Lungs accept their oxygen without trembling.
Feet stand inside their foot shapes, inside shoes someone has sewn.

We close the eyes of the dead so they will not see their not-seeing.
Light falls on the retinas' stubbornness, on pupils refusing to turn
        toward or away.

Fireflies, furnaces, quicksilvers fill them, cities & forests glinting
        though already finished,

And the tongues, the faithless tongues, continue speaking,
as lovers will, because they still love, long past the hour there is
        nothing left to say.

Engraving: World-tree with an Empty Beehive on One Branch

A too beautiful view rejects the mind.
It is like a person with a garrulous mouth but no ears.

When Bashō finished his months of walking,
he took off his used-up sandals,
let them fall.

One turned into the scent of withered chrysanthemum,
the other walked out of the story.

It's only after you notice an ache
that you know it must always have been there.
As an actor is there, before he steps in from the wing.

Another of Bashō's haiku:
a long-weathered skull, through whose eyes grow tall, blowing grasses.

They look now into a photograph,
a scraped field in France, September 1916:
men bending, smoking, gleaning the harrowed rucksacks for letters.

War, walking, chrysanthemum, sandal, wheat field, bee smoke of
    camera lens, war.

They're in the past, yet we just keep traveling toward them, then away,
carrying with us the remnant, salvageable,

refugee honey.

(No Wind, No Rain)

No wind, no rain,
the tree
just fell, as a piece of fruit does.

But no, not fruit. Not ripe.
Not fell.

It broke. It shattered.

One cone's
addition of resinous cell–sap,
one small–bodied bird
arriving to tap for a beetle.

It shattered.

What word, what act,
was it we thought did not matter?

On the Fifth Day

On the fifth day
the scientists who studied the rivers
were forbidden to speak
or to study the rivers.

The scientists who studied the air
were told not to speak of the air,
and the ones who worked for the farmers
were silenced,
and the ones who worked for the bees.

Someone, from deep in the Badlands,
began posting facts.

The facts were told not to speak
and were taken away.
The facts, surprised to be taken, were silent.

Now it was only the rivers
that spoke of the rivers,
and only the wind that spoke of its bees,

while the unpausing factual buds of the fruit trees
continued to move toward their fruit.

The silence spoke loudly of silence,
and the rivers kept speaking
of rivers, of boulders and air.

Bound to gravity, earless and tongueless,
the untested rivers kept speaking.

Bus drivers, shelf stockers,
code writers, machinists, accountants,
lab techs, cellists kept speaking.

They spoke, the fifth day,
of silence.

Page

It waits now for snows to fall
upward, into a summer
whose green leaves
still vanish,
but back into branch, into sap, into rain.

It waits for the old
to grow young, fed and unfearful,
for freighters to carry their hold-held oil
back into unfractured ground,
for fires to return
their shoe boxes of photos and risen homes.

It unbuilds the power line's towers
before the switch can be toggled,
puts the child, rock still in hand, back into his bed.

A single gesture of erasure
pours back into truck and then river
the concrete wall,
unrivets the derrick,
replenishes whale stocks and corals.

And why not – it is easy – restore the lost nurse herds
of mammoths to grazing,
the hatched pterodactyl to flight?
Let each drowned and mud-silted ammonite once again swim?

One by one unspoken, greed's syllables, grievance's insult.
One by one unsewn, each insignia's dividing stitch.
One by one unmanufactured,
unimagined: the bullet, the knife, the colors, the concept.

Reversal commands: undo this directional grammar of subject and
  object.
Reversal commands: unlearn the alphabet of bludgeon and blindness.
Reversal commands: revise, rephrase, reconsider.

And the page, malleable, obedient, does what is asked.

My Confession

Immortal soul, I did not believe in you.

Against the age's preference,
I wanted for your markings and history
the markings and history of, say, a small zebra—

slightly implausible, far from unique,
one visible pelt meant to disappear into the crowded many,
one dark stripe alive among the crowded many.

You seemed to want to go on separately.
You seemed to want elsewhere, and more.

I wanted less. One moment to pause
while setting kibble out in a dish for the calico cat
who might or might not
be inside the box when it finally opens.

One goldfinch holding the whole Mesozoic discovery,
hunting for seeds and hungry,
escaping, a few moments longer, the cat also hungry.

This dilemma cannot be solved,
and will be.

My immortal soul, perhaps you went into an *Archelon ischyros*,
swimming with its sea-turtle nose above water,
then diving.

Immortal soul, had you existed,
what more than that cold water could we have wanted?

Ghazal for the End of Time

(after Messiaen)

Break anything – a window, a piecrust, a glacier – it will break open.
A voice cannot speak, cannot sing, without lips, teeth, lamina propria
    coming open.

Some breakage can barely be named, hardly be spoken.
Rains stopped, roof said. Fires, forests, cities, cellars peeled open.

Tears stopped, eyes said. An unhearable music fell instead from them.
A clarinet stripped of its breathing, the cello abandoned.

The violin grieving, a hand too long empty held open.
The imperial piano, its 89th, 90th, 91st strings unsummoned, unwoken.

Watching, listening, was like that: the low, wordless humming of being
    unwoven.
Fish vanished. Bees vanished. Bats whitened. Arctic ice opened.

Hands wanted more time, hands thought we had time. Spending time's
    rivers,
its meadows, its mountains, its instruments tuning their silence, its deep
    mantle broken.

Earth stumbled within and outside us.
Orca, thistle, kestrel withheld their instruction.

Rock said, Burning Ones, pry your own blindness open.
Death said, Now I too am orphan.

Mountainal

This first-light mountain, its east peak and west peak.

Its first-light creeks:
Lagunitas, Redwood, Fern. Their fishes and mosses.

Its night and day hawk-life, slope-life, fogs, coyote, tan oaks,
white-speckled amanita. Its spiderwebs' sequins.

To be personal is easy:
Wake. Slip arms and legs from sleep into name, into story.

I wanted to be mountainal, wateral, wrenal.

My Debt

Like all
who believe in the senses,
I was an accountant,
copyist,
statistician.

Not registrar,
witness.

Permitted to touch
the leaf of a thistle,
the trembling
work of a spider.

To ponder the Hubble's recordings.

It did not matter
if I believed in
the party of particle or of wave,
as I carried no weapon.

It did not matter if I believed.

I weighed ashes,
actions,
cities that glittered like rubies,
on the scales I was given,
calibrated
in units of fear and amazement.

I wrote the word *it*, the word *is*.

I entered the debt that is owed to the real.

Forgive,
spine-covered leaf, soft-bodied spider,
octopus lifting
one curious tentacle back toward the hand of the diver
that in such black ink
I set down your flammable colors.

ACKNOWLEDGEMENTS

The author is deeply grateful to the MacDowell Colony, the Robert Rauschenberg Foundation's Captiva Island Residency, and Yaddo, under whose generous hospitality many of the poems in this book were written. Also to the journals and anthologies in which poems in this book first appeared, sometimes in slightly different versions:

Alaska Quarterly Review: 'Brocade', '*Fecit*', 'Musa Paradisiaca', 'Questionnaire'; *Alta:* 'Cold, Clear', 'Paint'; *Ambit:* 'My Glasses'; *The American Poetry Review:* 'Chance darkened me.', 'Corals, Coho, Coelenterates', 'Like Others', 'My Dignity', 'My Glasses'; *The Atlantic:* 'Lure', 'The Paw-paw'; *Australian Book Review:* 'Interruption: An Assay'; *Brick:* 'The Bowl', 'A Moment Knows Itself Penultimate', 'You Go to Sleep in One Room and Wake in Another'; *The Cortland Review:* 'You Have Not Decided'; *Guernica:* 'Practice'; *Mānoa:* 'A Bucket Forgets Its Water'; *The Massachusetts Review:* 'Without Night-shoes'; *Michigan Quarterly Review:* 'The Bird Net', 'Falcon', 'A Folding Screen'; *The New Republic:* 'Homs'; *The New Yorker:* 'Ants' Nest', 'Husband', 'I wanted to be surprised.', 'Things Seem Strong', 'Wild Turkeys'; *The New York Review of Books:* 'Day Beginning with Seeing the International Space Station and a Full Moon Over the Gulf of Mexico and All Its Invisible Fishes', 'My Confession'; *The New York Times Sunday T Magazine:* 'Engraving: World-tree with an Empty Beehive on One Branch'; *Noon: The Journal of the Short Poem:* 'Haiku: Monadnock', 'Notebook', 'A Strategy', 'Without Blinking'; *Orion:* 'Cataclysm'; Plume: 'I Said', 'Kitchen', 'Pelt', 'Snow', 'Words'; *The Plume Anthology of Poetry:* 'Advice to Myself', 'An Archaeology'; *Poetry:* 'Amor Fati', 'Harness', 'Wood, Salt, Tin.', 'Mountainal', '(No Wind, No Rain)', 'Page'; *Poets.org / Academy of American Poets Poem a Day:* 'Dog

Tag', 'Let Them Not Say', 'My Doubt'; *Salamander:* 'Now a Darkness Is Coming'; *The Southern Review:* 'Almond, Rabbit', 'A Ream of Paper'; *Spillway:* 'She Breathes in the Scent'; *Terrain.org:* 'Spell to Be Said Against Hatred', 'Today, Another Universe'; *The Threepenny Review:* 'Capital: An Assay', 'In A Former Coal Mine in Silesia', 'It Was as if A Ladder', 'Library Book with Many Precisely Turned-down Corners'; *The Times Literary Supplement:* 'Ledger', 'My Debt', 'Vest'; *Tin House:* 'Branch', 'In Ulvik'; *The Washington Post:* 'On the Fifth Day'; *Washington Square:* 'As if Hearing Heavy Furniture Moved on the Floor Above Us', 'To My Fifties'; *World Literature Today:* 'Biophilia', 'Bluefish', 'Description', 'O Snail', 'Obstacle', 'Sixth Extinction'; *Zyzzyva:* 'Some Questions'.

Poems have also been reprinted in the following anthologies, newspapers, and journals:

ANTHOLOGIES: *Best American Poetry 2019* (Scribner, 2019): 'Ledger'; *Fire and Rain: Ecopoetry of California* (Scarlet Tanager Books, 2019): 'Today, Another Universe'; *Ghost Fishing: An Eco-Justice Poetry Anthology* (University of Georgia, 2018): 'As If Hearing Heavy Furniture Moved on the Floor Above Us'; *Healing the Divide: Poems of Kindness & Connection* (Green Writers Press, 2019): 'The Bowl'; *Lightning Strikes II* (Dolby Chadwick Gallery, 2019): 'Mountainal'; *The Poetry of Capital* (University of Wisconsin Press, 2019): 'Capital: An Assay'; *Resistance, Rebellion, Life: 50 Poems Now* (Knopf, 2017): 'Let Them Not Say'; *America, We Call Your Name* (Sixteen Rivers Press, 2018): 'Let Them Not Say'; *Ways of Hearing* (Princeton University Press, 2020): 'Ghazal for the End of Time'; *What Saves Us: Poems of Empathy and Outrage in the Age of Trump* (Northwestern University Press, 2019): 'Let Them Not Say', 'On the Fifth Day'.

REPRINTS IN NEWSPAPERS AND JOURNALS: *The Irish Times:* 'On the Fifth Day'; *Frankfurter Allgemeine:* 'On the Fifth

Day' (translated); *Leaping Clear:* 'Spell to Be Said Against Hatred', 'Today Another Universe'; *Mānoa:* 'Some Questions'; *Marsh Hawk Review:* 'Amor Fati'; *The National: Amtrak Onboard Magazine:* 'Interruption: An Assay'; *The New York Times* (nytimes.com online feature): 'Let Them Not Say'; *The New York Times Magazine:* 'Mountainal'; *Poetry International Online:* 'Wood. Salt. Tin.', 'My Confession'; *Plume:* 'Amor Fati', 'Harness', 'Wood. Salt. Tin.'; *Salon:* 'Let Them Not Say'; *San Francisco Chronicle:* 'Let Them Not Say'.

'Ghazal for the End of Time' was commissioned for *Ways of Hearing* (Princeton University Press) by Princeton University Concerts, in honor of its 125th anniversary in the 2019/20 season.

'The Bowl' and 'Like Others' appeared as Tangram limited edition letterpress broadsides.

Eleven poems from this book appeared in *A Kerosene Beauty: Twelve Environmental Elegiacs*, a limited-edition letterpress hand-bound volume with original mezzotints by Holly Downing. Published by Nawakum Press in 2016, the eight copies not yet sold burned in the October 2016 Tubbs Fire, at that time the most destructive in California history.